The Sinking of the USS Indianapolis

by Marc Tyler Nobleman

Content Adviser: Thomas Saylor, Ph.D.,
Department of History,
Concordia University

Reading Adviser: Rosemary G. Palmer, Ph.D.,
Department of Literacy, College of Education,
Boise State University

COMPASS POINT BOOKS
MINNEAPOLIS, MINNESOTA

Compass Point Books
3109 West 50th Street, #115
Minneapolis, MN 55410

Visit Compass Point Books on the Internet at *www.compasspointbooks.com*
or e-mail your request to *custserv@compasspointbooks.com*

On the cover: Detail of *Twilight of Perseverance*, painting by Mark Churms.

Photographs ©: *Twilight of Perseverance*, detail of the painting by Mark Churms, 2001, All Rights
Reserved, cover, 28–29; Prints Old & Rare, back cover (far left); Library of Congress, back cover;
Corbis, 4; Bettmann/Corbis, 6, 8, 9, 36; National Archives and Records Administration, 7, 24; J.R.
Eyerman/Time Life Pictures/Getty Images, 11; Squalus Memorial Benefit Concert Program/Lane
Memorial Library, Hampton, New Hampshire, 12; U.S. Navy/National Archives and Records
Administration/Naval Historical Foundation, 13, 19, 31; U.S. Marine Corps/Naval Historical
Foundation, 15; Ralph Morse/Time Life Pictures/Getty Images, 17; U.S. Navy/Time Life Pictures/Getty
Images, 20; Brandon Cole/Visuals Unlimited, 26; U.S. Air Force, 32; The Granger Collection, New
York, 33; Marie Hansen/Time Life Pictures/Getty Images, 34, 35; Najlah Feanny/Corbis Saba, 37;
AP/Wide World Photos/The Indianapolis Star/Adriane Jaeckle, 39; AP/Wide World Photos/Darron
Cummings, 40.

Editor: Julie Gassman
Page Production: Noumenon Creative
Photo Researcher: Svetlana Zhurkin
Cartographer: XNR Productions, Inc.
Library Consultant: Kathleen Baxter

Creative Director: Keith Griffin
Editorial Director: Carol Jones
Managing Editor: Catherine Neitge

Library of Congress Cataloging-in-Publication Data
Nobleman, Marc Tyler.
  The Sinking of the USS Indianapolis/ by Marc Tyler Nobleman.
    p. cm. — (We the people)
  Includes bibliographical references and index.
  ISBN-13: 978-0-7565-2031-1 (hardcover)
  ISBN-10: 0-7565-2031-2 (hardcover)
  1. Indianapolis (Cruiser)—Juvenile literature. 2. World War II, 1939–1945—Naval Operations,
American—Juvenile literature. 3. Shipwrecks—Pacific Ocean—Juvenile literature. 4. McVay, Charles
Butler, d.1968—Juvenile literature. I. Title. II. We the People (Series) (Compass Point Books)
  D774.I5N63 2006
  940.54'5973—dc22   2006006768

TABLE OF CONTENTS

Secret Cargo

On July 16, 1945, the U.S. government tested an atomic bomb in a desert in New Mexico. The blast was so powerful that the sand beneath it melted into glass. This was the first time humans had set off a nuclear explosion.

The atomic bomb was set off at 5:29 A.M., filling the early morning New Mexico sky with a tremendous fireball.

Few people knew about the testing. Even the development of the bomb was kept a secret from most of the military, the country, and the world.

World War II had been raging since 1939. Though the fighting had ceased in Europe earlier in 1945, the war was not over yet. More conflict lay ahead in Asia. The United States planned to drop the atomic bomb on Japan and hoped that would be the final act of the war.

The same day as the testing, a warship named the USS *Indianapolis* departed from San Francisco, California. The ship was headed to a U.S. base on the island of Tinian in the West Pacific Ocean. The reason was mysterious. In San Francisco, under guarded watch, a heavy metal canister and a wooden crate 5 feet (1.5 meters) high, 5 feet wide, and 15 feet (4.6 m) long had been loaded into a secure area of the ship.

Not even the ship's captain, Charles Butler McVay III, knew what was inside the containers. A respected military man, McVay did not even ask. He had orders, and he was going to follow them.

Traveling at a record speed, the *Indianapolis* covered 5,000 miles (8,000 kilometers) in 10 days. On July 26, the ship arrived at Tinian. Though the island was small, it was the site of the world's largest airbase at the time. Eventually, the *Indianapolis* crew would learn

Captain Charles Butler McVay

how significant its mission was. The ship's secret cargo held parts for "Little Boy," the world's second atomic bomb. In the coming weeks, Little Boy was assembled on Tinian, then dropped by plane on Hiroshima, a Japanese city. This devastating act, along with another atomic bombing on Nagasaki, Japan, killed more than 100,000 people and ended World War II.

Naval Commander A.F. Birch, who helped develop the atomic bomb, labeled part of Little Boy prior to assembly.

The delivery of Little Boy was the first time that the *Indianapolis* became part of history. The second time also started with secrets and ended with death.

A WARSHIP IN PEACETIME

The USS *Indianapolis* was a warship built in Camden, New Jersey, during a time of peace. The 610-foot-long (186-m) ship was named for the capital of Indiana. It was put into service in 1932, 14 years after the end of World War I and seven years before the start of World War II.

In wartime, the ship served as a weapon with her

The Indianapolis *sped from Camden, New Jersey, to Rockland, Maine, as part of her trial cruise. After completing the trip successfully, she was commissioned.*

President Roosevelt shook hands with the ship's captain, John Morris Smeallie, as the Indianapolis *sailed to Washington, D.C., from Canada in 1933.*

giant guns. But before that, she was a symbol of American strength. President Franklin D. Roosevelt chose the *Indianapolis* as his ship of state, meaning his personal transport. Roosevelt took the *Indianapolis* on a "good neighbor" tour to South America in 1936. This marked the first time a

9

U.S. president traveled beyond North America while in office.

The *Indianapolis* was a cruiser, a ship that is smaller than a battleship and bigger than a destroyer. In battle, cruisers sailed alongside the larger battleships. The larger ships targeted enemy ships and land forces with their gigantic guns, while the cruisers shot at enemy planes. Cruisers were also intended to draw enemy fire and escape quickly.

The steel armor of the *Indianapolis* was between 2 and 4 inches (5 and 10 centimeters) thick, compared to an average battleship, which had 13 inches (33 cm) of protection. The thinner armor allowed the *Indianapolis* to travel at high speed. But it also made her much more vulnerable to damage if attacked.

By the time the United States entered World War II in 1941, the *Indianapolis* was no longer state of the art. Newer cruisers had better armor and traveled faster than the 9-year-old ship. Still, the Navy had wartime plans for the *Indianapolis*, and the ship was put on active duty in 1942.

Two Hits After Midnight

After delivering the parts for Little Boy in July 1945, the *Indianapolis* left Tinian and made a brief stop in Guam, a nearby island and U.S. territory. From there, she prepared to sail for the Philippine island of Leyte, 1,500 miles (2,400 km) west of Tinian. The *Indianapolis* was one of the

The harbor at Guam was often filled with U.S. ships during the summer of 1945.

ships that would participate in a planned invasion of Japan, so she was moving into position.

Before leaving Guam, Captain McVay requested an escort ship for the trip to Leyte. While he did not know if enemy submarines were in the vicinity, it was standard procedure for a larger ship to accompany a cruiser for protection. The *Indianapolis* did not have the equipment needed to detect submarines, but a destroyer did. No other American ship had been forced to cross the Philippine Sea without an escort during the entire war. But Captain Oliver Naquin, McVay's superior, said no to the request.

Only days before, on July 24, a Japanese submarine had sunk a destroyer escort near the route the *Indianapolis* would take to Leyte. Also cause

Captain Oliver Naquin

The Japanese submarine I-58 *was state of the art, with two 4,700-horse power engines that pushed it through the water at impressive speeds.*

for alarm, a top secret Navy code-breaking system called ULTRA had located yet another Japanese submarine named the *I-58* operating in that region.

Naquin knew about both situations, yet he did not tell McVay. The ULTRA program was so top secret that only officers above a certain rank were told about it, and Captain McVay's rank was not high enough. Also, the U.S.

military did not want to fire on every Japanese sub it discovered, because the Japanese might then realize that the United States could crack their codes. Therefore, on July 28, McVay left for Leyte without realizing the full extent of the danger his ship might face.

On the evening of July 29, the *Indianapolis* was zigzagging. In this defensive maneuver, ships moved in a Z pattern, rather than a straight line, in an attempt to avoid torpedo strikes from submarines. According to the sailors of the *Indianapolis*, the sky was overcast. The captain was authorized to stop zigzagging at night if visibility was poor. McVay gave that order but said the ship should resume zigzagging if the clouds cleared. Soon after, he went to bed.

Meanwhile, from his nearby submarine, Japanese Lieutenant Commander Mochitsura Hashimoto spotted the *Indianapolis*. His sub was the *I-58*—the very one that the ULTRA system had located.

Hashimoto could not tell what style of ship the *Indianapolis* was, but he knew it was not Japanese. Five

The torpedo room of the I-58 was used for the storage, handling, and firing of torpedoes.

minutes after midnight on Monday, July 30, he fired six torpedoes. Four of them missed. The other two ripped into the right side of the *Indianapolis*.

STRANDED AT SEA

The impact of the torpedoes was so forceful that the ship actually rose out of the water and spun in a slightly different direction. The first torpedo blew off the front of the *Indianapolis*. The second hit the middle near a fuel tank. The explosions split the remains of the ship in two. Ocean water rushed into the jagged front opening. The damaged ship chugged forward and drooped below the surface of the water at the same time. Flames tore at the ship, and smoke clogged the sky.

Much of the *Indianapolis* lost electrical power and radio contact, but the crew was able to send out distress signals. Naval stations on Leyte received a message that the *Indianapolis* had been torpedoed. The Navy also picked up and translated a message from the *I-58* stating that the sub had sunk an American vessel.

However, the Navy did not send help to the *Indianapolis*. An officer on Leyte responded to a distress

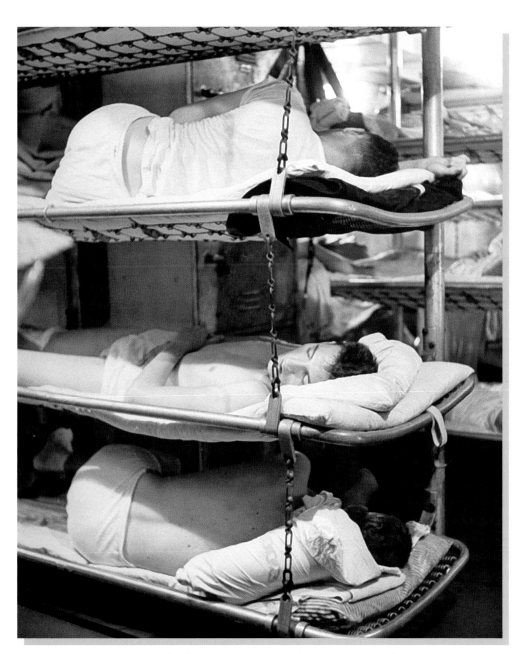

Many of the 1,196 men on the ship were sleeping in bunks similar to these when the torpedoes hit.

signal but did not get a reply. According to Navy regulations at the time, distress signals were considered real only if they could be confirmed. Also, naval officers may have believed the Japanese messages were tricks to lure American ships into a Japanese ambush.

Meanwhile, Captain McVay knew that the *Indianapolis* was going down, and he gave the order to abandon ship. Because the speakers and amplifier of the public-address system were out, he had to spread the word by shouting. About 300 men had already died in the explosions or by drowning. The surviving crew members, approximately 900 men, plunged into the open sea—about 300 miles (480 km) from the nearest land.

Some jumped, some slipped, and some were pushed. Some areas of the ship had sunk so low that men simply stepped into the ocean with barely a splash. About half the men were wearing life preservers. Crew members got 12 of the ship's 35 life rafts into the water. Everyone was shocked, afraid, and confused.

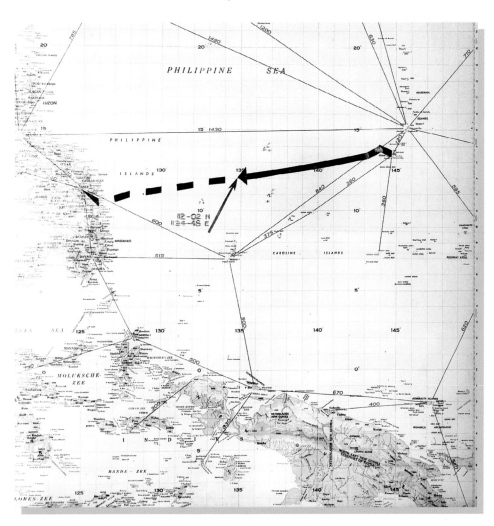

A historic chart shows the ship's route from Guam to the disaster site.
Dashed lines show the intended route to the Philippines.

As the *Indianapolis* broke apart, her rear tipped
almost straight up. The crew frantically dog-paddled away.
If they stayed close to a sinking ship, they could be sucked

underwater. Some turned to watch their cruiser slide into the sea. Nose first, the ship fell through 3½ miles (5.6 km) of water into pitch blackness. Bodies, debris, and churning foam floated in its place.

The crew's beloved "Indy" was no more than a memory in just 12 minutes.

Only 12 minutes had passed since the torpedoes hit.

The *Indianapolis* was scheduled to dock in Leyte the next day, July 31. At the time, naval officers did not have to report the arrival (or nonarrival) of all ships—only the noncombatant ships, meaning those ships that did not take part in armed conflicts. This rule was created to limit the amount of paperwork officers had to do. Of course, the *Indianapolis* was a combatant ship.

The officers in charge of tracking the movement of ships were busy. When the *Indianapolis* did not arrive as expected, the Navy marked her as "overdue," not lost. They did not send a search party.

Yet, out in the rough sea, 900 men were praying that they would.

HUNDREDS OF SHARKS

The crew of the *Indianapolis* was lost at sea. Screams sounded over the rolls of the waves. Most of their food and water was gone, and many men were burned or injured. The water was thick with black fuel oil from the ship. It covered the crew members so that only their eyes and mouths were visible. It got in their mouths and caused some to vomit.

The long, cool night gave way to a hot day. In the light, they could see there were hundreds of survivors. But the men were scattered across several miles of ocean. Many tied themselves closely together, but the currents carried some away from the main group.

Men without life preservers clung to those who had them. When a man died, another took his life preserver. The life preservers generally worked well, but after about 48 hours in the water, some became waterlogged. The men would then sink into the water up to their chins and struggle to keep their heads up.

U.S.S.R.

Korea

JAPAN

CHINA

• Hiroshima

Nagasaki

ASIA

San
Francisco • NORTH
AMERICA

AFRICA

AFRICA

Pacific Ocean

AUSTRALIA

SOUTH
AMERICA

Okinawa

Pacific Ocean

Philippine
Islands

USS *Indianapolis*
disaster site

Tinian

Guam

N
W   E
S

Leyte

0   250   500 miles

0   250   500 kilometers

The USS Indianapolis *went down hundreds of miles from land.*

    Crew members without hats grew dizzy from
the exposure to the sun. Though the oil coating them
stung their eyes and smelled foul, it prevented sunburn.
Many wore only pants, and some had no clothes at all.

23

Even if they were in a life raft, the men's bodies and minds suffered severely.

Even though the air was warm, their body temperatures began to drop from being in the water so long.

The men divided up what little unspoiled food and water they found drifting among the wreckage. Their thirst was intense. Their mouths dried out, and their tongues swelled up. The saltwater grew more and more tempting, but they knew it was harmful to drink. Some did anyway. It worsened their condition, and they began to suffer extreme physical and mental pain.

Soon the men began to see things that were not really there. Sometimes whole groups of men had the same hallucination. In one case, a group swam off one night and came back the next morning, claiming that the *Indianapolis* had not sunk. They said they had been aboard her all night, drinking water and milk. Other men believed them and swam off with them. They were never seen again. Another time, men began to line up in the water because they believed there was an island up ahead and they could each have a turn resting for 15 minutes.

Of all the hardships, perhaps the most unthinkable were the sharks. Hundreds of them began to circle the men the first day they were in the water. At first, the sharks fed on those who were either dead or separated from the group. Then the sharks got bolder and randomly attacked people in the larger clusters.

"It seemed like the sharks were smart," survivor Lyle M. Pasket later recalled. "They stayed outside the

Many men saw sharks swimming around their feet or circling around them.

perimeter most of the time. Then when these fellows hallucinated ... they thought they'd seen this and that over there. ... We tried hauling back into a group, but that was taxing our strength. So we just had to let them go. They would never come back; but we could hear them scream and you know the sharks got them."

The crew of the *Indianapolis* had begun their service in the war battling the enemy. They ended their service battling thirst, hunger, exhaustion, fear, cold, sharks, and, for some, insanity.

"MANY MEN IN THE WATER"

As the days stretched on, the men remained hopeful. Some even had the stamina to try to save their fellow men from drowning. But the stress was too much for others, who unfastened their life preservers and gently slipped beneath the water.

Everyone wondered why it was taking the Navy so long to save them. They had seen military planes flying overhead every day. But the pilots were too high up to see people bobbing in the ocean. And since the Navy still did not list the *Indianapolis* as missing, the pilots did not know to look for anyone.

The *Indianapolis* had sunk in the early morning of Monday, July 30. At 11:25 A.M. on Thursday, August 2, help finally arrived. Lieutenant Chuck Gwinn was piloting a small plane, scouting for Japanese subs. By chance, he noticed a long patch of oil in the water and flew in for a closer look. Only then did he see the men. He did not know they were from the *Indianapolis*—or even if they were American. He radioed for help, describing "many men in the water."

Another naval pilot, Lieutenant Adrian Marks,

The USS Basset *(in background), a transport ship, also came to aid in the rescue.*

was sent to the scene. On the way, he communicated with Captain Graham Claytor, whose destroyer, the USS *Cecil J. Doyle,* was 200 miles (320 km) from the *Indianapolis* crew. Without orders, Claytor turned his ship around and

headed toward the survivors.

Marks arrived hours before Claytor and began to drop rafts to the men from his plane. But sharks attacked again, so Marks made a drastic decision.

Disobeying Navy regulations, he landed his large plane on the surface of the ocean. From there, he and his crew pulled *Indianapolis* crew members from the water. When the inside of the plane got too crowded, they tied survivors to the wings with parachute cords. Marks saved 56 men.

The sky was dark when Claytor arrived. Even though enemy subs might see his ship, he aimed search-lights at the water. A survivor recalled that seeing the searchlights gave him and others hope. "Then it started to pour rain. ... And it just rained like the devil, so we put a tarp over our head ... That was our first drink of water we had in about four days."

The *Cecil J. Doyle* saved close to 100 men. More ships and planes arrived. Although the search for others

Survivors were stretched out on the beach at Guam to wait for transport to a hospital.

would continue until August 8, the last survivors, including Captain McVay, were pulled to safety on Friday, August 3. Of the 1,196 crew members of the *Indianapolis*, 317 had survived.

THE CAPTAIN'S NEXT ORDEAL

On August 6, the United States dropped the atomic bomb called Little Boy on Hiroshima. Three days later, a second atomic bomb was dropped, this time on Nagasaki. Having suffered massive destruction and loss of life, Japan surrendered.

After Little Boy was dropped, smoke billowed 20,000 feet (6,100 m) over Hiroshima.

On August 15, the end of World War II was announced in huge headlines. The same day, the sinking of the *Indianapolis* quietly made the news in the United States.

The crew of the *Indianapolis* did not blame Captain McVay for the disaster—but the Navy did. Four months

The New York Times.

"All the News That's Fit to Print"

LATE CITY EDITION

VOL. XCIV..No. 31,980.

NEW YORK, WEDNESDAY, AUGUST 15, 1945.

THREE CENTS

JAPAN SURRENDERS, END OF WAR!
EMPEROR ACCEPTS ALLIED RULE;
M'ARTHUR SUPREME COMMANDER;
OUR MANPOWER CURBS VOIDED

HIRING MADE LOCAL

Communities, Labor and Management Will Unite Efforts

6,000,000 AFFECTED

Draft Quotas Cut, Services to Drop 5,500,000 in 18 Months

Third Fleet Fells 5 Planes Since End

ALL CITY 'LETS GO'

Hundreds of Thousands Roar Joy After Victory Flash Is Received

TIMES SQ. IS JAMMED

Police Estimate Crowd in Area at 2,000,000— Din Overwhelming

PRESIDENT ANNOUNCING SURRENDER OF JAPAN

YIELDING UNQUALIFIED, TRUMAN SAYS

Japan Is Told to Order End of Hostilities

Notify Allied Supreme Commander and Send Emissaries to Him

MACARTHUR TO RECEIVE SURRENDER

Formal Proclamation of V-J Day Awaits Signing of Those Articles—Cease-Fire Order Given to the Allied Forces

SECRETS OF RADAR GIVEN TO WORLD

Its Role in War and Uses for Peacetime Revealed in Washington and London

PETAIN CONVICTED, SENTENCED TO DIE

Terms Will Reduce Japan To Kingdom Perry Visited

TREATY WITH CHINA SIGNED IN MOSCOW

Hirohito on Radio; Minister Ends Life

Two-Day Holiday Is Proclaimed; Stores, Banks Close Here Today

World News Summarized

Cruiser Sunk, 1,196 Casualties; Took Atom Bomb Cargo to Guam

MacArthur Begins Orders to Hirohito

The war's end overshadowed the sinking of the USS Indianapolis. *The New York Times* ran a small story on the ship far under large headlines about Japan's surrender.

33

McVay's trial was the first time in U.S. history that a captain had been court-martialed for losing his ship as the result of an act of war.

after the sinking, McVay was court-martialed. The Navy accused him of two errors—failing to zigzag, which was supposedly the reason the *Indianapolis* was hit, and failing to abandon ship fast enough.

The survivors and others thought the Navy was trying to hide its own mistakes. Even several higher-ranking officers did not think McVay should be court-martialed. He did not break naval rules. His orders had given him the right to stop zigzagging when the weather was not clear.

At the trial, the Navy brought Japanese officer Mochitsura Hashimoto to the United States to testify against McVay. Yet Hashimoto did the opposite. He said that he could have hit the *Indianapolis* even if the ship had been zigzagging.

Mochitsura Hashimoto took an oath before testifying at McVay's court-martial.

Some of the survivors were called to serve as witnesses at the trial.

Many of the case's facts were not brought to light during the trial. No one discussed that the Navy knew Japanese subs were detected in the region. No one discussed why the Navy did not give the *Indianapolis* an escort as McVay requested. No one discussed why the Navy neglected to notice immediately that something had gone horribly wrong with the *Indianapolis*. If these facts had come up, they would have revealed that other naval officers were more responsible for the tragedy than McVay.

McVay was found not guilty of abandoning the ship too late, but guilty of failing to zigzag. The judgment meant he would no longer be allowed to command a ship. Instead, he was given a job in a naval office. For years, families of sailors who died sent him hostile letters saying that it was his fault. By 1968, McVay could no longer handle the grief, and he took his own life.

Before McVay died, his fellow *Indianapolis* survivors had begun a campaign to prove that their captain was innocent. As the years passed, a number of other people joined them, notably Florida Representative Joe Scarborough, New Hampshire Senator Robert Smith, and an

Senator Robert Smith

37

11-year-old boy from Florida named Hunter Scott, who turned a school project on the *Indianapolis* into a quest for justice. Even Hashimoto, who had become a Shinto priest in Japan, wrote a letter to the U.S. government in support of McVay.

In 2001, the Navy made an official statement that it no longer blamed Captain McVay for the loss of the *Indianapolis* or any of its crew. This did not erase the conviction for failing to zigzag from McVay's record. But the men who served under him felt that his name was finally cleared.

SURVIVORS AND HEROES

The sinking of the *Indianapolis* resulted in the largest loss
of life from a single incident in the history of the U.S.
Navy. As the public heard the story, many people called the

*Survivors marked the 60th anniversary of the ship's sinking with a parade
through downtown Indianapolis, Indiana.*

crew heroes. The crew members, however, did not think of themselves that way. In their own minds, they were simply survivors. History will remember them as both.

Survivor Albert Morris in front of an outdoor monument in Indianapolis, Indiana, that honors the fallen crew members

For four days, the men of the *Indianapolis* were adrift in the ocean with little nourishment, little protection, and no guarantee of rescue. They had the added hardship of watching others suffer. Most of them were in their late teens or 20s at the time. The trauma of the experience haunted them for the rest of their lives.

Every two years, the survivors meet in Indianapolis to remember their fallen comrades. On the 60th anniversary of the sinking, 93 of the 317 survivors were still alive. Even into their 80s, the men of the *Indianapolis* had nightmares about the night they lost their ship, their friends, and nearly their own lives.

Glossary

atomic bomb—a highly powerful bomb that can cause widespread damage

conviction—a decision that a person is guilty of a criminal act

court-martialed—put on trial for breaking military law

distress signals—calls for help

hallucination—the experience of hearing or seeing things that are not really there

maneuver—a strategic military movement

testify—to give information under oath during a trial

visibility—the degree to which surroundings can be seen clearly

vulnerable—capable of being harmed

warship—a military ship designed for combat

World War II—a conflict from 1939 to 1945 in which the Allies (including the United States, the United Kingdom, France, and the Soviet Union) defeated the Axis (including Germany, Japan, and Italy)

DID YOU KNOW?

- The USS *Indianapolis* was about as long as two football fields. The ship contained a dentist's office, a post office, a bakery, a library, and a photo lab.

- The Pearl Harbor naval base in Hawaii was the home port of the *Indianapolis* when the Japanese attacked it on December 7, 1941, but the ship was not there at the time.

- On March 31, 1945, during the U.S. invasion of Okinawa, Japan, a kamikaze plane flew itself into the *Indianapolis*, killing 13 men. Fearing the wrecked plane could explode, officers pushed it off the ship into the ocean. The *Indianapolis* went to San Francisco for repair, then left from there for what would be its final voyage.

- Hunter Scott, the junior high student who worked to clear Captain McVay's name, conducted two years of research and interviewed nearly all of the remaining *Indianapolis* survivors. One naval historian said Scott put together "the greatest collection of information on the USS *Indianapolis* in the world."

IMPORTANT DATES

Timeline

1932	The USS *Indianapolis*, a navy cruiser, is put into service.
1936	President Franklin D. Roosevelt tours South America on the *Indianapolis*.
1945	On July 26, the *Indianapolis* delivers parts of an atomic bomb from the United States to Tinian in the West Pacific Ocean; on July 30, the *Indianapolis* is sunk by a Japanese submarine, losing all but 317 of her crew; in December, Captain Charles McVay is court-martialed and convicted of failing to zigzag.
1960	Survivors of the *Indianapolis* disaster hold their first reunion, which McVay attends.
1968	McVay commits suicide after years of receiving hate mail from families of the *Indianapolis* sailors who died.
2001	The U.S. Navy announces that McVay will no longer be held to blame for the loss of the USS *Indianapolis* or members of her crew.

Important People

W. Graham Claytor Jr. (1912–1994)
Captain of USS Cecil J. Doyle, *a destroyer that changed its course to come to the aid of the survivors of the* Indianapolis; *prior to the war, he worked as a lawyer*

Wilbur "Chuck" Gwinn (?–1993)
Lieutenant who was the first to spot the survivors of the Indianapolis *floating in the ocean during a routine patrol mission; his radioed messages were the first cause for alarm regarding the lost* Indianapolis

Mochitsura Hashimoto (1909?–2000)
Lieutenant commander of the Japanese submarine that sank the Indianapolis, *who later joined the effort to clear Captain McVay's name; following the war, he became a priest of the ancient Japanese Shinto religion*

Charles Butler McVay III (1898–1968)
Captain of the USS Indianapolis *on her final voyage; was later court-martialed by the Navy and found guilty of failing to zigzag; he was well-liked by his crew for his confident yet easy-going manner*

WANT TO KNOW MORE?

At the Library

Chrisp, Peter. *The War in the Pacific*. Austin, Texas: Raintree, 2004.

Harris, Nathaniel. *Hiroshima*. Chicago: Heinemann Library, 2004.

Lawton, Clive A. *Hiroshima: The Story of the First Atom Bomb*. Cambridge, Mass.: Candlewick Press, 2004.

Marquette, Scott. *World War II*. Vero Beach, Fla.: Rourke Publishing, 2003.

Nelson, Peter. *Left for Dead: A Young Man's Search for Justice for the USS Indianapolis*. New York: Delacorte Press, 2002.

Sheehan, Sean. *World War II: The Pacific*. Milwaukee: World Almanac Library, 2005.

On the Web

For more information on the *sinking of the USS* Indianapolis, use FactHound to track down Web sites related to this book.

1. Go to *www.facthound.com*

2. Type in this book ID: 0756520311

3. Click on the *Fetch It* button.

Your trusty FactHound will fetch the best Web sites for you!

On the Road

The USS Indianapolis
National Memorial
The north end of Canal Walk
Indianapolis, IN
An outdoor memorial to the final
crew of the USS *Indianapolis*

Indiana War Memorial Museum
431 N. Meridian St.
Indianapolis, IN 46204
317/232-7615
A museum honoring Indiana's
veterans from all American wars

Look for more We the People books about this era:

A complete list of We the People titles is available on our Web site:
www.compasspointbooks.com

INDEX

About the Author

Marc Tyler Nobleman is the author of more than 50 books for young people. He writes regularly for *Nickelodeon Magazine* and has written for The History Channel. He is also a cartoonist whose single panels have appeared in more than 100 international publications, including *The Wall Street Journal*, *Good Housekeeping*, and *Forbes*. He lives with his wife and daughter in Connecticut.